Contents

Throwing away clothes

Everybody needs clothes. As the world's population grows, the demand for clothes increases and this means that more raw materials are needed to make them.

The racks of clothes in shops often tempt people to buy clothes they don't really need. A surprising number of clothes are never worn.

More clothes

People in developed countries usually have more clothes than those living in developing countries. However, many of the clothes on sale in developed countries are made in parts of the world where salaries are lower.

Among the largest clothes manufacturing countries are China and Pakistan. Clothes from these countries in the developing world have to be transported thousands of kilometres to shops in the developed world.

Dealing With Waste

OLD CLOTHES

Sally Morgan

FRANKLIN WATTS
LONDON • SYDNEY

First published in 2006 by
Franklin Watts
338 Euston Road
London NW1 3BH

Franklin Watts Australia
Level 17/207 Kent Street
Sydney, NSW 2000

Produced for Franklin Watts by White-Thomson Publishing Ltd
210 High Street,
Lewes BN7 2NH

Editor: Rachel Minay
Designer: Brenda Cole
Picture research: Morgan Interactive Ltd
Consultant: Graham Williams

Picture credits
The publishers would like to thank the following for reproducing these photographs:
Alamy 16 (Frank Vetere); Corbis 6 (Jose Luis Pelaez, Inc.), 17 (Musa Farman/EPA); Ecoscene
front cover main image (Vicki Coombs), 7 (Chinch Gryniewicz), 8 (Christine Osborne), 9 (Stephen
Coyne), 10, 11 (Christine Osborne), 13 (Vicki Coombs), 14, 15, 18 (Ed Maynard), 19 (Eric
Needham), 23 (Latha Raman); Imagestate 27 (SO/GRANDEUR NATURE/HOA-QUI); i-stockphoto
front cover top right (Vaide Dambrauskaite); Emmeline 4 Re 20 (Mick Eason); Recyclenow.com
front cover bottom right; Traid 12 (Darrell Fields), 21 (Vladimir Jansky), 22 (Alessandra Rigillo),
26 (Alastair Guy); Vision Aid Overseas 24 (Brian Donnan), 25 (Paul Constant).

British Library Cataloguing in Publication Data
A CIP catalogue record for this book
is available from the British Library.

ISBN: 978 0 7496 6436 7

Dewey classification: 363.72'8

Printed in China

Franklin Watts is a division of Hachette Children's Books, an Hachette Livre UK company.

Clothes waste

It is estimated that the average life of a garment in some countries is just three years. Fashion is always changing, so people are always buying new clothes. Also, children grow out of clothes and shoes very quickly. People do not mend or alter clothes as much as in the past. Instead they are thrown away and replaced with new ones. As a result, clothes and shoes make up about 3% (by weight) of a typical bin in the UK or USA. Most of this is taken with the rest of the rubbish to landfill sites where it is buried.

In this book you will read about the different types of fibres used to make clothes and how clothes can be reused and recycled.

It's my world!

How far have the clothes in your wardrobe travelled? Look at the labels and see which countries they were made in. Have any been made in your own country? Look at a world map to try and work out how far the clothes have been transported.

In the developing world, it is more common for people to buy fabric and make their own clothes. In this Kenyan market, fabrics are hanging up on display.

Materials for clothes

Textile is the name given to any type of material that is made from fibres or threads. There are many different types of textiles. They include woven, knitted, crochet and knotted textiles as well as non-woven ones, such as felt.

Plant fibres

Plant fibres that are used to make textiles include cotton and linen. Cotton fibre comes from the fluffy white seed heads of the cotton plant. A plant called flax is used to make linen. Fibres found in the stem of the plant are made into thread and then woven into linen fabric.

Artificial fibres

Over the last 40 years or so a range of artificial fibres has been used to make clothes. These include nylon, rayon and polyester. These fibres are made from oil. The artificial fibres can be used on their own to make clothes, or mixed with natural fibres. For example, cotton fabric is very comfortable to wear but it creases easily and needs to be ironed. This can be overcome by weaving polyester into the fabric. Polyester cotton does not crease as much or shrink after washing as much as clothes made from 100% cotton. The different per-centages of fibres that the item of clothing is made from will be written on the label.

Cotton fibres are found in the seed heads of cotton plants. This cotton farm worker in Turkey is removing the seed heads. In some parts of the world this is done by machine.

The bark of the rubber tree is cut so that a white liquid called latex oozes out. This is collected and treated to make rubber.

Wool, leather and rubber

The fleece of animals is made into textiles, too. For example, wool comes from sheep; angora and cashmere come from goats. In addition, there are materials such as leather and suede, which come from the skin of an animal such as a cow. Rubber for shoe soles is taken from the latex of rubber trees.

It's my world!

Read the labels in your clothes and see what fibres were used to make them. Some fabrics may be a blend between a natural fibre and an artificial one, for example, polyester cotton.

9

Making textiles

All clothes – whether they come from natural or artificial fibres – have an impact on the environment during their manufacture.

Crops and animals

Most farmers spray crops such as cotton and flax with pesticides to kill pests. However, some pesticides may kill useful insects such as bees and ladybirds. They spread fertilizers on the soil to make sure the plants have enough nutrients and water them during dry weather. Sometimes the fertilizers drain off the soil into rivers where they cause water pollution.

Sheep, goats and cattle eat food and they produce waste in the form of dung. Also animals may be sprayed with chemicals to keep flies and other pests away.

Did you know...?

About 0.5 kg of cotton is needed to make a T-shirt. To obtain this cotton about 120 g of pesticides may have been sprayed on the cotton plants and 15 litres of water used to wash the cotton. A further 175 litres of water will have been used in the dyeing process.

Cotton plants are attacked by many pests, such as the cotton bollworm, so the cotton fields have to be sprayed with pesticides many times during the growing season.

From fibres to fabric

The raw materials are taken to factories where they are washed using a lot of water, a valuable but sometimes scarce resource. The cotton or wool is spun to make a yarn. This may be bleached to lose its colour or it may be dyed with chemicals to give it a specific colour. These processes create a lot of waste water. It is too dirty to be allowed to drain into rivers or the sea so it has to be treated first. The yarn is then transported to factories where it is woven into different types of fabric. The fabric is then sold to clothing manufacturers who cut it up into pieces to make clothes. Then the garments have to be packaged and transported to shops.

Artificial fibres

Artificial fibres, such as nylon and polyester, are produced in a factory. This uses up electricity and valuable raw materials, such as oil and water. There may be harmful waste products, such as nitrous oxide, from the manufacture of nylon. This gas cannot be allowed to escape into the atmosphere as it contributes to global warming.

Whichever type of fibre a garment is made from, at all of these stages in its manufacture energy is used and waste is produced.

The fibres of cotton are taken to a textile factory where they are carded (lined up) and made into a soft untwisted rope called a sliver, which is spun to make a yarn.

Reduce, reuse and recycle

To manage waste, we need to reduce, reuse and recycle. Reduce means to cut down on waste created, for example during clothes manufacturing. Reuse means to put something to a new use. Recycle means to use something again.

Old clothes can be washed and taken to a clothes bank for recycling.

Did you know...?

More than 70% of the world's population regularly wear second-hand clothes.

Reducing clothes waste

Reducing the waste means that clothes manufacturers have to create less waste during the manufacturing process. Sometimes the waste fibres are collected and put back into the yarn-making process. When the fabric is cut up to make up a garment there are lots of leftover bits. They can be used to make the stuffing for furniture and mattresses.

Reusing clothes

Reusing clothes can mean passing clothes onto other people such as family or friends. Alternatively, unwanted clothes can be sold in a second-hand shop or car boot sale or given to a charity shop or jumble sale. Charity shops use the money raised from the sale of clothes for good causes. Any clothes that do not sell or are too worn to be reused are recycled instead.

Recycling clothes

Recycling clothes means to reclaim the fibres from clothes that have no further use and to make them into new clothes. Recycling is very efficient as most of a garment can be recycled (see pages 18–19). Clothes can also be altered or adapted so they can be used again. Designer garments and unique accessories can be made from recycled fabrics (see pages 20–21).

Second-hand clothes, books and household goods can all be sold in charity shops and the money from the sales used for good causes.

Reusing clothes

It is important to try to reuse as many clothes as possible rather than throw them away. Sometimes it is possible to make a simple alteration to get more use out of a garment. Also, clothes can be passed on to somebody else.

Charity shops

Good-quality clothes can be taken to a charity shop where they can be sold. Shoes, boots and accessories, such as handbags and belts, can also all be sold. Most second-hand clothes are sold for between £2 and £10 per item, but some clothes could get £100 or more. This means that a tonne of clothing can earn anything between £1,000 and £10,000.

It's my world!

How many clothes in your wardrobe have been passed to you from a brother or sister? Have you altered any of the clothes to make them fit?

These racks contain quality second-hand clothes. They have been sorted according to type and size and will be transported to shops where they will be sold.

These clothes have been collected via clothes banks. Each item will be checked and graded for quality.

Sorting and grading

In most developed countries there is a network of clothes banks where people can take their unwanted garments, curtains, bedlinen and shoes. The contents of these clothes banks are taken to sorting centres where experienced workers sort through the clothes. The workers have to identify the type of textile quickly and grade it according to its quality. The best clothes are sent to charity shops. Other wearable clothes are sent overseas. The rest is sent for recycling – about one-quarter of what is collected. The main markets for European second-hand clothes are African countries, Pakistan, and Estonia, Latvia and Lithuania. The USA and Canada tend to send clothes to South America, Africa and Pakistan, whilst Australia and New Zealand usually send clothes to Vietnam, Thailand and Malaysia.

Clothes aid

After a natural disaster, such as an earthquake, volcanic eruption, hurricane or flood, there is an urgent need for clothes. People who have lost their homes and belongings need emergency supplies of clean clothes, toiletries and nappies for babies.

Collecting and sorting

Often emergency clothes collection points are set up where people can take their clothing donations. Then the clothes have to be sorted by volunteers who remove unsuitable or tatty, old clothing that nobody would want to wear. Once the clothes have been sorted they can be shipped by air to the disaster area.

In 2005, Hurricane Katrina (a powerful storm) devasted New Orleans and the surrounding area in the United States. Immediately people across the United States collected clothes and other items to help people who had been made homeless by the hurricane.

Types of clothes

Clothes are needed in a full range of sizes. Useful items include underwear, shoes and sensible clothing such as shirts, trousers and jumpers. People usually throw their underwear away rather than recycle it, but second-hand underwear is in great demand after a disaster.

Different climates

Waterproof coats and wellington boots may be needed if it is a wet climate, while blankets, thick coats, scarves and gloves are needed in mountainous or northern areas where there is cold weather. Baby and children's clothing is also needed.

After the earthquake in Pakistan in 2005 many thousands of people were left homeless. They needed warm winter clothing. This young girl is sitting on a pile of donated clothes.

Did you know...?

On 8 October 2005 a strong earthquake hit the mountainous regions of Pakistan-administered Kashmir and killed 73,000 people. More than 2.5 million people were left homeless. The area has extremely cold winters so the main priority of the aid organizations was to transport winter tents, blankets, warm clothing and food into the devastated area before the roads serving the remote villages were cut off by snowfalls.

Recycling clothes

If clothes cannot be reused then they can be recycled. Recycling clothes is very efficient and the specialist companies who do this can recycle as much as 95% of most clothes, so very little goes to waste.

All of these curtains, sheets and clothes can be recycled. Sheets can be cut up into wiping cloths while any towels and blankets may be shredded for stuffing.

Wiping cloths

Almost any fabric can be recycled. Cotton and silk are often used to make wiping cloths for a range of industries from cars to mining, and for use in paper manufacture. White fabrics are particularly useful. It is far better to recycle fabrics in this way than for people to buy disposable wipes, which are used once and thrown away.

Flocking

Garments such as trousers and skirts are sold for flocking. The garments are shredded and used as fillers for car insulation, roofing felts, furniture padding and mattresses. Sometimes the flocking is used as carpet underlay or for soundproofing panels.

Reclaiming fibres

Woollen garments are sent for fibre reclamation. They are sorted according to colour and then the threads are unravelled and made into new clothes. Rags and other items of fabric that are too damaged to be used for clothes or for threads can be shredded and used as shoddy (a woollen fabric made from rags), felt or padding and stuffing.

It's my world!

How many different ways could you recycle an old sheet? It could be cut up to make new pillowcases or cut into squares for cleaning cloths. It could be made into a carrying bag for shoes or into a linen bag for dirty washing. Can you think of any more ways?

There are many benefits from recycling clothing. Less waste ends up in landfills and fewer new clothes are needed so fewer resources and raw materials are used to make them.

The household waste in this Spanish rubbish tip contains many clothes and old shoes that could have been recycled.

New clothes from old

Some old clothes can be remade into new clothes. There are even specialist companies that make designer clothes from recycled cloth.

Designer clothes

There are clothes designers in many countries who specialize in making desirable designer clothes from quality second-hand clothes. A pair of plain blue jeans for example can be transformed into an individual designer item by hand painting designs onto the denim or a long-sleeved dress can be changed into one with no sleeves. They also use quality second-hand cashmere and angora to make high-quality new jumpers.

An amazing range of clothes and jewellery can be made from the old clothes that are put into clothes recycling banks.

Buttons and bows

Buttons can be removed from old clothes and used on new ones. Decorative bows can be made from strips of colourful material. Strips of fabric can also be made into fabric flowers that could be used to decorate a jacket or suit.

New shoes

There are companies that make shoes from a wide variety of recycled textiles. One company makes shoes from old blankets, leather, men's suits, the silk from parachutes and towels. The soles are made from recycled rubber.

Unique clothes

A clothes shop has racks of the same style of garment in different sizes and colours. Recycled clothes are different. Every garment is a handmade original or 'one-off' and nobody else will have one exactly the same.

Each item that this model is wearing is unique and has been made from recycled clothes or boots.

It's my world!

Rather than throw clothes away, see if you can alter them so you can wear them again. Try updating an old jumper by adding a patchwork of different fabrics. Buttons, bows made from recycled lengths of fabric or a piece of lace can alter the appearance of a shirt, jacket or jumper. Fabric bags can be made from an assortment of fabrics. You can get some ideas by visiting some of the websites of designers who specialize in making clothes from recycled fabrics.

Developing world

Often people in the developing world cannot afford to buy new clothes so they have to use second-hand ones. Women are taught to sew and they can take the cloth from old clothes and make new items out of it.

Shoes and boots

Shoes and boots can be reused or recycled, too. Often shoes are in good condition, particularly children's shoes, as they grow out of them rather than wear them out. Wellington boots may develop a leak so they cannot be worn but the rubber can be recycled.

These old shoes have been taken to a recycling centre where they will be sorted according to size. The better-quality shoes will be sold or sent overseas.

Shoe banks

The best way to recycle old shoes and boots is to tie the pairs together and take them to a shoe bank. The shoes are collected and taken to recycling centres.

Sorting and selling

As with clothing, shoes and boots have to be sorted. The good-quality shoes and boots can be sold in charity shops or sent to developing countries where quality shoes are in short supply. For example, good-quality sports shoes are very expensive in Bangladesh so young people cannot afford to buy them. This means that they have to play in unsuitable footwear that does not protect their feet, such as open-toed sandals.

This man in India is taking apart old shoes so that the valuable parts, such as the rubber sole and the leather, can be reused.

Recycling old shoes

Even very old shoes can be recycled, too. In many developing countries, the rubber soles from old shoes are removed and stuck on new shoes. Some manufacturers of sports shoes collect old shoes. The rubber soles are removed and ground down into granules. The granules can be used to make sports surfaces.

It's my world!

How many pairs of shoes and trainers do you own? Do you wear them all? Raw materials and energy are used to make shoes so make sure you recycle your old shoes so the materials can be used again.

Old glasses

Millions of people in the developed world wear glasses to correct their sight. However there are as many as 200 million people in the developing world who see everything through a blurry haze. All they need is a pair of glasses.

This tailor in Burkina Faso needed a pair of glasses so that he could see to carry out his job of making clothes.

Reusing glasses

Just like second-hand clothes, old glasses can be either reused or recycled. There are many opticians and charities that collect old glasses. Any pairs that have broken frames are removed. The quality glasses are then cleaned. They are then sorted according to the strength of the lenses. Any broken frames made of metal can be recycled. The metal is sent to recycling plants where it will be melted down and reused.

This Ethiopian man is having his eyes checked. He will be given a pair of glasses to correct his eyesight.

It's my world!

Do you or your family have any old pairs of glasses lying in a drawer? You may not be using them because your prescription has changed, but they may be useful to someone living in a developing country. Find out if your local optician collects old glasses.

Restoring eyesight

Second-hand glasses can be shipped to developing countries where they are needed by people with poor eyesight. Some charities send out teams of opticians who train local people to give eye tests. Patients are given a pair of glasses that match their prescription.

The way ahead

Everybody can help to reduce the growing quantities of clothes, shoes and accessories that are thrown away each year. It is also important to think about how the fabrics are made and to reduce the amount of waste created in the manufacturing process, too.

This model is wearing clothes that have been made from recycled fabrics.

Sustainable fibres

Textiles made from cotton, wool, linen and other natural fibres are described as being sustainable. This is because the crops can be replanted or more animals bred so there is a continuous supply of the raw materials into the future. Textiles made from rayon or polyester come from oil, which is an unsustainable raw material. Fossil fuels such as oil, gas and coal are being used up at a far more rapid rate than they are being made so the supply will run out. Scientists estimate that there is just 30 to 50 years supply of oil left. So by choosing natural fibres you can help to reduce the use of fossil fuels.

Environmentally friendly fibres

Organic cotton is grown without the use of pesticides and chemical fertilizers. The yields are lower but there is less damage to the environment. Unbleached cotton also causes less harm, as the fibres are not treated with chemicals and less waste water is produced in the manufacture.

Hemp – the way forward

Hemp is a very useful crop that can be used as a fuel and to make paper, plastics and fabrics. Until the 1820s it was used to make about 80% of the textiles in Europe and North America. It was also the main oil used in lights before the arrival of electricity. Slowly its use declined as it was replaced by cotton and oil. However, it is being rediscovered and the amount of hemp grown in the world is increasing once again. This crop could be grown to provide a sustainable source of oil and fibres.

Hemp grows to about 2 m in height and the long fibres, shown here, come from the stem. Steam is used to separate out the fibres from the stem.

It's my world!

What can you do?

▸ Think before you buy new clothes – do you need to buy something or can you make do with what you have already got in your wardrobe?

▸ Update your clothes by adding buttons, lace or patchworks or use some fabric paint to give them a fresh look.

▸ Buy from second-hand shops or charity shops. You can save money and help the environment and a charity at the same time.

▸ Never throw textiles in the bin, even small items, as they can all be recycled. Wash the textiles and take them to the nearest clothes bank.

▸ Recycle shoes and boots, too.

▸ Take old glasses to an optician so they can be reused or recycled.

Glossary

Developed country

a country in which most people have a high standard of living

Developing country

a country in which most people have a low standard of living and who have poor access to goods and services compared with people in a developed country

Fertilizer

a source of nutrients sprayed onto soil to supply plants with all their requirements for growth

Flocking

shredded textiles used for padding or filling

Fossil fuel

a fuel formed over millions of years from the remains of plants and animals, for example peat, coal, crude oil, and natural gas

Landfill

a large hole in the ground used to dispose of waste

Pesticide

a chemical that is used to kill pests such as greenfly

Recycle

to process and reuse materials in order to make new items

Reduce

to lower the amount of waste that is produced

Reuse

to use something again, either in the same way or in a different way

Sustainable

describes a resource that will not run out or can continue to be manufactured into the future without harming the environment

Textile

a material made from fibres or threads

Unsustainable

describes a level of use of a resource that cannot be maintained into the future and which will cause the resource to run out

Waste

anything that is thrown away, abandoned, or released into the environment in a way that could harm the environment

Yarn

spun fibres or thread, used in the production of textiles

Websites

Friends of the Earth

www.foe.org.uk

Website of the charity Friends of the Earth that gives information about campaigns, including those for encouraging recycling.

TRAID (Textile Recycling for Aid and International Development)

www.traid.org.uk/

TRAID raises money for international projects as well as promoting recycling and waste reduction in the UK. Unwanted clothes that are donated are hand sorted or redesigned and reconstructed to make new recycled garments, and sold through TRAID's charity shops.

Tokyo Recycle Project

www.powerhousemuseum.com/tokyorecycle/

An exhibition that is being shown around the world on the work of Masahiro Nakagawa, designer of the popular Japanese streetwear label 20471120. Instead of creating new garments from scratch, Nakagawa and his team of recyclers breathe new life into old and worn garments.

United States Environmental Protection Agency

www.epa.gov

This website has lots of environmental information on all issues, not just waste. There is an EPA Kids Club (www.epa.gov/kids) with information on waste and recycling.

Vision Aid Overseas

www.vao.org.uk/

Website of the UK charity that is dedicated to helping people in the developing world whose lives are affected by poor eyesight, particularly in those cases where glasses can help.

Waste Online

www.wasteonline.org.uk

Comprehensive website looking at all aspects of recycling.

Every effort has been made by the publisher to ensure that these websites are suitable for children and contain no inappropriate or offensive material. However, because of the nature of the internet it is impossible to guarantee that the contents of these sites will not be altered. We strongly advise that internet access is supervised by a responsible adult.

Index